A Weekly Reflection

Musings for the Year

Robin Fennelly

A Weekly Reflection
Musings for the Year

Copyright © 2012 by Robin Fennelly

ISBN 978-1-105-41420-6

Cover Art: Caitlin Fennelly, M.F.A.

Bound and Printed in the United States

Dedication

In dedication to my Mother, Jeanne who provided a loving home and open environment to explore the varied spiritual paths.

In dedication to my Husband, Ned who has always supported my dreams and encouraged me to pursue my chosen path.

In dedication to my five wonderful Children, Kyle, Jenny, Eryn, Caitlin and Jessica who taught me patience and nurturing and allowed me the privilege of helping them find their own destinies.

In dedication to the Elders and community of like minded Spirits that is The Assembly of the Sacred Wheel where I have learned, taught and grown.

In dedication to the Adepts and many fine teachers of the diverse Spiritual Paths, who are I am honored to call Friend and who live the Truth that all Paths lead to the One.

Table of Contents

About A Weekly Reflection

I love to find new pieces of information that I can mull over. These often lead me down new paths of exploration where some of the most treasured inspirations have emerged. With that thought in mind *A Weekly Reflection: Musings for the Year* was crafted.

I chose the word "reflection" to inspire the idea that every piece of information, every event or action, every thought or feeling is somehow mirrored within our own being. This reflection often goes unnoticed until we take the time to pause and re-read, re-do or re-think.

As you move through the weeks with these musings and calls to action, be reminded that the greater inspiration we have is within ourselves. We have the gift of creativity, choice about how and where we express that creativity and who will receive benefit of our inspired actions.

Each week has a page following it entitled: *Notes From the Week*. Use this as a journal page to record your impression of the week's reflection and any insight you may have gained from spending some time musing about what was offered up.

My hope is that you will begin your own practice of staying alert to the many ways that inspiration present itself.

Blessings on your journey of a new year!.... RCF

WEEK 1: Be Spontaneous

To be spontaneous is to act without ego and enlist our sense of creativity and imagination. Choose a restaurant of different cultural foods. Choose bubblegum over your regular brand and test your childlike skill. Finger-paint! Anonymous -

How often, as adults do we allow ourselves the joy of being spontaneous? Children naturally allow their interest and actions to flow in unrestrained creativity. There is a freedom that occurs when you allow the restraints and structure to loosen a bit and open yourself to different opportunities. Taking these alternate paths can often inspire us to try something new, or engage in a way of being that would have otherwise gone unexplored.

Leave a little earlier and take a more scenic route to work. Call a friend you haven't seen in a while and set up a coffee date. Go out for a movie and dinner in the middle of the week instead of waiting for the weekend. Buy a box of crayons or markers and draw what is around you. Then, hang it on your refrigerator for all to see.

For this week, explore the inner child that is spontaneous, joyful and creative. Remember the sheer joy of losing yourself within the notes of a beautiful piece of music.

Where will your spontaneity take you?

Notes From the Week:

"Is the intention pure, selfless, and born out of love? Is it based on truth? Does it result in peace? If so, it is a right action."
Sai Baba -

I often come across various quotations that stir me deeply and bring me back to a place of remembrance of what my Higher purpose is. These are not something I look for; but rather, they present themselves at just the appropriate time. The quote above was posted on my daughter's social site, which I rarely look at. And, as soon as I read it, I knew this was my reminder to be more mindful of how I move through my day. To be more conscientious in my interactions and to pause before deciding, speaking or acting to allow for the space of observation to come forward. That briefest moment of reflection before charging ahead can reveal a different perspective, a deeper truth and possibly a different choice.

For me, the questions posed in this quote are the filters that should guide me to move from a place of love and greater understanding. They are a reminder of the great responsibility held in each of us that is the call to right action. And, the obligation to make each day an expression of integrity; acting in a way that is in alignment with my Soul's work.

What intention do you have? And, what filters will separate the true gold from that of the "fool"?

Notes From the Week:

WEEK 3: The Tabula Rasa

I was recently listening to music to use for a piece of choreography and came across something called the *Tabula Rasa* by Arvo Part. The music is crafted using a geometric structure of sound that repeats the same basic set of notes with minor variations and dynamics as the complete composition. The intriguing part is how the music winds around a central core of sameness.

Initially what attracted me to this piece of music was the title, "Tabula Rasa". The term in Latin equates to the English "blank slate" but originally comes from the Roman word, tabula or "a wax tablet", which was blanked by heating the wax and then smoothing it to give a tabula rasa. I liked this idea of mind being molded by experience and the many permutations that it may take on, while still operating from a central core of knowledge.

I believe this principle to be one that is a staple of spiritual progress. The idea that we allow our mind to periodically return to this state of the Tabula Rasa, the blank slate, as we inch along the Path. Each of these states of pause brings us to greater awareness of the process of mind and inspiration and the synthesized creation of something new from their union.

How will you make your mind The Tabula Rasa?

Notes From the Week:

WEEK 4: What's Your Style?

Regardless of the form your meditation practice takes, the important component is your desire to change your consciousness and bring yourself to a state of serenity, calm and inner awareness. As with any endeavor try to find those things that will keep you engaged in regular practice.

If you are highly visual, incorporate visual imagery either real or imaginary in your practice.

If you enjoy music and are easily transported to a space of calm by listening to specific music, add this as a background of focus (generally light classical, chant or music specific to meditation is best) or create your own music by chanting or reciting a specific mantra.

If movement is the key to bringing you balance and inner calm, try a walking meditation or a yoga practice that is structured towards meditative focus. And, if you simply want to sit, reflect and cultivate inner awareness and calm in any given situation find that quiet place within, follow your breath and then relax into a state of contemplation following your own path of stillness. Let yourself be guided by the images created on your inner screen of the subconscious mind and listen to the sound of your heart beat and the music of life beating within.

This week, experiment with different ambient settings and techniques to deepen your meditation practice.

Notes From the Week:

WEEK 5: Toning the Chakras

Vibration surrounds us and informs every cell of our being with its impact. Using vibration in a purposeful way can stimulate and awaken the subtle energies of our being. The practice of "sounding" the Sanskrit name of a specific chakra strengthens and gives greater flexibility to these sources of energetic filter.

The chakras are the primary energy vortices that interpenetrate our subtle bodies. They are continually receiving energy and emanating energy out.

A Bija Mantra is a sacred vowel tone that is vibrated to create a resonance with its corresponding chakra. In Sanskrit Bija means seed. Each of the sounds is thought to contain the essence of the universe and reveal the cosmological meaning of the type of energy to which it relates. The **a** is pronounced as in short vowel a = 'ah'. Let each of the tones roll off of your tongue as you tone them; giving pronounced length to each of the letters and finishing with the **m** = "hum" as its sound vibrates against the roof of your mouth.

Root = Lam
Sacral = Vam
Solar Plexus = Ram
Heart = Yam
Throat = Ham
Third Eye = Om
Crown = Silence

Try the Bija sounds daily this week as part of your meditation practice.

Notes From the Week:

WEEK 6: The Path of Service

The idea of service is one that has long been held as a guiding force in the following of the path I have chosen. As all seekers do, I have gone through varying stages of development and coinciding with those birthing pains and joys has come a predictable chameleon like energy around my definition of "service". This changeability of definition seems to be the natural result of the transformation and growth that occurs as you move forward on any spiritual path.

As your perception of the world around and within you changes, the ideology you develop around how and what a path of service looks like re-forms that perception, and consequently your actions in accord with the more expansive view.

Recently, I have found it increasingly difficult to clearly define what this deep yearning that I have to be of "service" looks like. The actions I have taken to answer this call need a closer look and a renewed sense of purpose. I will dig deeply this week to give more clarity to this desire to serve and perhaps through those efforts the opportunities that have gone unnoticed will be more clearly seen?

How will you define your path of service to others?

What will be your path of service to yourself?

Notes From the Week:

WEEK 7: The Great Investment

We are all teachers as we move through this human existence. Some are formally trained and dedicated to that career, others teach as an avocation. But, the greater majority unknowingly instruct, guide and set example as they go through their mundane activities.

If we think of each person we interact with as a student; one who is taking in the essence of how we carry ourselves, what we say and what our actions display, we become more mindful of what lessons and messages we are sending. Conversely, we ourselves are students within another's daily interactions. We pick up clues, both subtle and overt to what lessons that individual or group is sending out. They in turn become our teachers; investing in our progress and banking on our success.

As givers and receivers of the gifts, lessons and treasures of the interconnected nature of our existence, let us "bank" on the investment of a positive nature, make our withdraws on those things of inspiration and generously deposit into a lifetime savings of "interest" in mankind.

What will your deposits be this week?

Notes From the Week:

WEEK 8: Digging In

Dig your fingers deep into the earth
Fertile granules of life and decay
Tiny bits of energy darting here and there.

Life force moves down submerged
Appendage and roots beginning
To weave intricate pathways
Towards the heart of the Great Mother.

How deeply do you extend your roots into this place of home- Earth? We are supported and surrounded by a living breathing world, and for most the fast paced day marches on with barely a thought given to the surface upon which we walk.

As you walk through the city streets, look down and perhaps find the joy in seeing a single small flower sprouting upward between blocks of cement. As you look out from your office window, look up at the sky and any birds that wing their way across its backdrop.

Go outside just after a snowstorm and listen to the echo of snowflake. Walk among the trees and look up through branches that stretch and reach. Look out across the waters of pond, lake or even city fountain and see the reflection mirrored back of what stands above. Dig your energetic roots down deep into the belly of the earth and draw up the energy of sustained life. Where will you dig a little deeper this week?

Notes From the Week:

WEEK 9: Honoring the Cycles

We are nearing the end of Winter's hold, although depending on where you reside geographically it may seem as though Spring is very far off.

In keeping with the cycles of nature these past months of cold, snow and moving indoors has offered great opportunity for slowing down and turning to the quiet and stillness within. I began thinking about how this is exactly what I have craved during these past few months.

My body and mind in rhythm with the external cycles of nature has sought out ways to make me more mindful of moving through the day in a more serene, calm and more focused manner. I've wanted to curl up with a good book and just stay inside; warm, cozy and completely "at home" with myself. So now that Spring is just as few weeks away ~ March 20th ~ I'm anxious to see what those times of moving within- both physically and spiritually- have made fertile ground for. With the advent of Spring the world is aglow with potential. What has lain dormant throughout the winter is now ready to be quickened and brought forth to be enjoyed by all.

It may already be Spring or Summer where you are, but the idea remains the same. Finding ways to honor the energy of the seasons and honor yourself in connecting with those energies. How will you attune to the cycles of nature this week?

Notes From the Week:

WEEK 10: The Truth

Each day we awaken to our worlds of sight, touch, and the sounds that clamor for our attention and response. Each day we strive to achieve and move forward and do so in such an utterly complicated and circuitous way that we return each evening tired and drained from our exertions. When, in truth, the way is simple and the obstacles we face and disconnectedness we feel are of our own making. Slow down. Open yourself to moving through your day in a new and simpler way.

Seeing is the Truth when eyes grow blind and all that was hidden is seen in its true clarity.

Feeling is the Truth when every sinew, muscle and bone longs for the touch of that which is held in the memory of endless time.

Words are the truth when they are the sacred echoes carried on the winds of transformation.

And of all the truths we have power to claim as our own;

Love is the ultimate Truth that when given freely and unconditionally unifies all in its embrace. For in its simple truth lay the true nature of what is the entirety and source of everything.

What Truths do you hold as your own?

Notes From the Week:

WEEK 11: Engaged in the Surroundings

A recent sitting at a local Starbucks, sipping coffee and having my journal and pen nearby inspired a piece of writing. I had simply chosen to sit, observe and allow whatever muses of inspiration presented to guide my way. Had I been engrossed in reading or surfing the web, I would have missed the energy and activity that was evolving outside the window where I sat. Life, untold stories and moments of inspiration are continually around us. How much or how little we choose to acknowledge these moments is within our control. Our lives are filled with an over abundance of technology. Cell phones, portable computers and blue tooth devices have, for many, become the primary means of connecting and staying in constant touch with others. Although each of these devices has multiple benefits, they have also served to dis-engage and dis-connect us. There is certain joy to be savored in the act of sitting across from another, having a deep and meaningful conversation that is not in danger of being interrupted by a text or call. There is meaningful energy in taking the time to select a special piece of paper or card, to write a heartfelt message and then have it received and carefully opened with curiosity and the recipient's energetic imprint now mingling with that of the sender on the paper. There is great reward in sitting quietly and gazing out at others of humanity without distraction, being fully engaged in the activity all around. Connect in a meaningful way this week.

Notes From the Week:

WEEK 12: The Small Joys

We are continually reminded to take note of those blessings in our lives that would otherwise remain unnoticed. The gentle smile of a stranger or precious time spent offering a kind word or act of encouragement and support.

We are told of the treasures that are to be found in stilling the mind and sitting simply and quietly in devotion to Deity. We are praised for selfless acts and move at times with the skill and precision of a surgeon in removing obstacles for those less fortunate than ourselves.

We offer up words of praise, comfort and inspiration and never skip a beat when speaking up for justice and equality. And, although these endeavors span far and wide they are still, nonetheless, only a fraction of measure of the joys we receive in kind from the Divine.

If you fill the space of your being with each of these "small" joys we eagerly offer to others in the name of God or Goddess, community or individual you will have built the bridge of foundation that connects to the very heart of the Divine. This bridge holds the expanse of heavenly gaze, the breadth of earth-filled beauty and the return to the joy of Spirit within that blazes brightly when fed by the gifts of service.

What small joys will you offer and receive this week?

Notes From the Week:

"All that is gold does not glitter, not all those who wander are lost. The old that is strong does not wither, deep roots are not reached by the frost. From the ashes a fire shall be woken, a light from the shadows shall spring. Renewed shall be the blade that was broken, the crownless again shall be king."
- J.R.R. Tolkien, The Lord of the Rings -

Within every action, thought and endeavor is a paradox. Something that is in contradiction to what the surface appearances are presenting. This is the "maya" of illusion that is spoken of in the Eastern philosophies.

When we accept anything at face value and don't take a closer look at where the untruths lay, we become sheep that blindly follow wherever they are led. Taking the time to dig a little deeper, then question and test the boundaries of what is present often gives more insight into what the resulting course of action will be.

Finding the hidden meaning. Revealing the truths that are just within reach. Acknowledging the importance of everything no matter how small and seemingly unimportant. Parting the veil and fully embracing the reality that surrounds me. This is my work. This is my quest and this is where I will find the most transformational lessons.

What will you acknowledge as paradox and what greater truth will you reveal?

Notes From the Week:

Inspired by a day at *The Wolf Sanctuary* **in Litiz, PA.**

I have seen the beauty of winter, the turning
of the leaves and the greening of the woods
as summer takes its hold.

I have run with my family and moved silently through
densely carpeted forest floor seeking my prey.
I have called to my young and heard the music
Of my clan echo through the woods.

I have hunted and fought to claim my territory.
I have found sanctuary in my new home from
A world that is quickly diminishing mine.

And, as I look out at human faces eager to
know more of my stories and wild nature
I question which of us being held captive.

Reflect this week on the wildlife that shares our world.
Acknowledge the varied gifts they offer to humanity
and the lessons they have for us about our own place in
the world.

Perhaps, give thought to how you may offer up your
service to an animal shelter or sanctuary.

Notes From the Week:

WEEK 15: Visualize This!

Being able to call up in detail specific images is a good skill to develop, both for spiritual/magickal practice and also as a tool for memory and mundane activities. Spend this week practicing this basic candle-gazing practice to develop your visualization skills.

Sit comfortably with a lit candle approximately 18 inches away from you. A tall white pillar candle works well for this or a taper in a 2-3" candle holder. Try not to use a tea light or flat candle as you don't want to have to tilt your head and gaze down while doing this exercise. Relax with a few concentrated breaths and allow your gaze to soften while staring at the candle. Begin by taking in the image of the entire candle and its holder. Then, draw your gaze in and up towards the lit wick and the blue white flame. Hold this point of gaze for several minutes. Then, close your eyes. You should be able to recreate the outline of the flame and light. Try to hold this image on your inner screen as long as possible. In the beginning, it is natural for it to dissipate, but with practice you will experience a lengthening of the time you can hold the image with clarity and greater detail behind closed eyes.

When you have mastered doing this with the candle in front of you, begin to practice conjuring up the image without the candle being there in physical form. How much of the image can you bring to life? You can vary this exercise by applying the basic technique to a selection of different objects.

Notes From the Week:

WEEK 16: The Space of Spiritual Practice

I sit in a place of quiet
And the tensions of the day
Fall like droplets of water at my feet.

Before me is a candle of light
That opens my mind to the
Potential that lay within.

Below me is the floor
Of my home, the
Strength and foundation
That supports and holds
Me in its warm embrace.

Above me is the shelter that
Keeps me warm and dry as
The elements rage and winter
Takes its icy hold.

I sit and I connect with
My innermost thoughts
And this sacred space
Holds my secrets and
With silent encouragement
Moves me along my chosen Path.

What is your space of spiritual practice?

Notes From the Week:

This week the focus is on engaging your senses more fully. For the most part, we go through our day unaware of the great pleasure and information being received from our five overt senses.

Sight: We live in a vastly visual world, surrounded by all manner of collage, color and scenery. Focus on a singular point of sight; a tree, building, etc. and take in every bit of detail. **Hearing**: Music, voices, technology and the drone of transparent white noise fill our sense of hearing. Be selective and tune into listening intently and fully to a conversation you are having or an inspiring piece of music. **Taste:** Take longer to chew the food you select to nourish your body. Indulge in the taste of something you consider to be a treat. Savor every morsel. See how long the taste will remain on your palate. **Smell:** Try a new cologne or perfume and see if you can pick out the keynote of the aroma. Engage your sense of smell more fully as you eat. Take in the aroma of the food before actually putting it into your mouth. This simple act will alert the taste buds that something good is coming their way. **Touch:** Reach out and touch an object or another person, focusing your awareness on the texture as it moves across your fingertips. Slow down and savor the feeling.

Select one or two of your senses and try to be fully aware of the subtleties of each. Enjoy each sensation.

Notes From the Week:

WEEK 18: The Holiday

As the established holiday seasons approach there is a greater opportunity for connecting more deeply with the roots that hold us steady in our everyday workings. The routines we establish for our daily living become more important as the irregularity of holiday preparations move us out of our comfortable routines. Finding alone time and time for renewal become luxuries as we seek to fulfill all of our commitments, remain active and social and enjoy the added time with family and friends.

We forget to give ourselves the gift of time and spaciousness. Time to renew. Time to reflect on those in our lives and those who have touched our lives in the past. Time to enjoy the bounty of the personal harvests we've reaped. And, most importantly, time to explore those gifts of ourselves that we may invest in the future of others.

We don't have to wait for a specific holiday to step into these gifts. We can create our own place of celebration for ourselves. Select a day and enjoy the holiday of "you".

Give yourself the spaciousness of your own day of celebration, rest and reflection this week.

Notes From the Week:

WEEK 19: Changes

Most of us resist change. Change is something to be feared. The unknown is disquieting and uncomfortable. The very word itself brings an overwhelming desire to dig in and hold on firmly to whatever is about to change. The irony is that most times after the change has occurred and time has settled in to bring a new perspective, we feel liberated from the old ways that held us inert. The fact of the matter is that change is continually occurring both within and without our being. The cells of our physical bodies shed, regenerate and change daily; transparently and without pain or discomfort. If they did not, our quality of health and life would be impaired.

Our environment changes daily. We encounter different people in different settings hourly. Even what we consider the routine of our job, changes in the scope and intensity that we bring to the task at hand; as well as what the contents of that task are.

Moving with the flow of these changes that are unnoticed, yet prevalent, is what moves us through one day to the next with minimal (if any) discomfort or fear at what lay in wait around the bend. The challenge is bringing this level of acceptance to those "unexpected" change-filled moments.

For this week, take note of how you respond to the subtle changes that occur daily. Formulate a plan to respond in the same way to those unexpected changes.

Notes From the Week:

WEEK 20: The Lunar Tides

With all the diverse energy and mystery surrounding the Moon is it any wonder that its greater mysteries are used to enhance sacred work. Dancing around a fire on a moon lit night and moving to the beat of rhythmic drums is the nearest one can come to being totally absorbed into the Natural world.

Working with the Moon and her phases are part of the Natural cycle that is used in the Craft of the Witch. We draw from the energy of the Goddess as represented in her various forms of Maiden, Mother and Crone and see these in manifest form as New (beginnings), Full (maturity) and Dark Moons (endings and release).

Our intuitive and emotional selves move with the changing of the lunar phases and accessing this energy can be transformational in connecting us more deeply to the many cycles of the seasons, the daily path of the Sun and our own life's passages as we move through the chronological years of aging.

This week do some research into the lore and fact of the moon's energy. See when the next New and Full moon occur and take note of the subtle undercurrents and changes of energy as the Moon moves from New (beginnings) to Full (most potent and fully developed).

Allow your emotions to move in accord with the natural cycles of the lunar phases and be open to greater insight and intensity in all your endeavors.

Notes From the Week:

WEEK 21: Sitting to Receive

During my lunch break I walked to my favorite space that is nestled within a bustling suburban community. As I sat quietly on the porch of the historic colonial home that was once farmland, I felt my body relax and allowed my mind to open to receiving whatever wished to present itself.

Streams of energy came pouring in related to recent studies of Alchemy, Qabalah, Tarot, Astrology and more. Esoteric writings, ownership of my spiritual and mundane practices and the many paths I have taken all came flooding in.

As I sat quietly allowing these things to move in and through me, all seemed to come to a point or place of convergence. I was aware that my physical self, acting as a receptacle was held within the support and greater container of the space of nature around me. The feelings of inter-connectedness resonated somewhere deep within me and my physical self, subtle bodies, physical space and nature's subtle bodies flowed together, each feeding and taking spiritual nourishment from the other. I don't know how long I sat in this way because time seemed to pause and there was nothing but interwoven energy, seamlessly and effortlessly moving. As the feeling subsided there was at once greater clarity and more detail in what I was externally looking at. Take some time this week to sit and reflect on the synthesis of your spiritual practice.

Notes From the Week:

A staple of spiritual work is keeping a journal. This offers opportunity to look back at early steps and progress made and pulls to the surface areas that may need more practice. Committing to writing those moments of inner reflection and change offers insight into the subtleties of what present as larger experiences.

I admit that I was reluctant at first, feeling that somehow I was taking precious time away from more reading and study. But, after a few weeks of dedicated effort to setting aside this valuable time to record, I was addicted to the process. Here are some tips to get you started.

- Select a journal that you absolutely love. It can be something as simple as a small spiral bound notebook or as elaborate as a finely crafted hand made writing journal.

- Personalize it in some way. This serves a two-fold purpose. First, it ensures that you will be using something that you enjoy using. And, secondly, when you engage a component that requires kinesthetic (the actual hands on of gluing, pasting, drawing, etc.) and thinking (selection of what will be your stamp of personalization) processes you have created an important energetic link to the object.

Purchase or create a journal that is uniquely yours. As you make the first entry, offer up a prayer of blessing that its writings inform this and all future work.

Notes From the Week:

WEEK 23: Ready, Set, Action!

I want "everything"! To do, to know, to learn, to be adept at everything! This has always been my nature and that hunger served me well in my youth, but has become cumbersome and limiting as I embrace my latter fifties. The reality is that there is just not enough time in a day, a year or a lifetime to make that an achievable or even productive goal.

This behavior colors all aspects of my life, but most notably the dynamics of my spiritual path have raised the efficacy of this need to a place front and center. I decided to use the point of half year as a marker for what has been accomplished, and what remains to be done.

Conversation with an Elder of our Tradition, a physical challenge and the resultant inner dialogue have helped to reign in this compulsive need to extend myself much further than I should and focus with intention on how and where my energies are distributed.

We get so caught up in the process of continual movement that we no longer see that we are not truly moving forward, but simply spinning our wheels, caught in the illusion of the moment.

So, ready, set, act with intent! Slow the pace and really savor the journey along the way. What progress does your half-year marker show?

Notes From the Week:

WEEK 24: Just Breathe

We breathe as an automatic physiologic function necessary to sustain life. We breathe deeply in relaxed moments and shallow and labored when stressed. It is a reflex that for the most part is not filled with intention or with any thought in mind other than necessity.

Developing awareness and control of the breathing process, is the foundation of most spiritual and energy work. The Four-Fold Breath is a common technique used in spiritual practice to provide greater relaxation and deeper breathing, resulting in fuller capacity of the lungs. This is an excellent way to begin a meditative session or use as way to relax into and open to the journaling process.

Begin by sitting in a quiet, comfortable setting. Focus your attention on the rhythm of your breath. As you begin to feel your body relax focus your attention more fully on your breathing.

Take a full deep breath- inhaling for a moderate count of 1-2-3-4. Hold this breath for a moderate count of 1-2-3-4.Exhale for a moderate count of 1-2-3-4.Hold at the completion of exhalation for 1-2-3-4.

You may continue to breathe in this manner for several sets of the four. Eventually, your breath will establish its own rhythm and attention to counts will not be necessary.

Try the Four-Fold Breath Technique daily this week.

Notes From the Week:

WEEK 25: Training the Mind

The Mind helps us to re-member and re-assemble the pieces that make up who we are, physically, emotionally and spiritually. The Mind is the place of manifesting and bringing those various parts of self selectively into the foreground where they can be used appropriately.

It is the birthing place of the inspired thought and the place of logic and reason. It is active and can be the greatest tool in pushing us forward towards our goals.

When we learn to control our mind we are on the path towards stepping into our full power. This Power is the knowledge and use of your own Divine nature. It is the key to controlling and developing your own energies and how they impact everything that makes up your world of experience. It is knowing when and how to exert your will so that it may work in alignment with the Higher Will and when to simply pause in stillness and be guided by your Higher nature which is in constant communication with the Universal Mind that is the source of all life.

Make note this week of your thoughts and the consequences and actions as a result of giving those thoughts power. What would you change or how would you bolster your mind's creations?

Notes From the Week:

WEEK 26: Music for the Soul

I grew up in a household that loved quality music. There was always an opera to listen to, classical music on records or TV shows that were musical in entertainment. This love of music supported my endeavors to train as a classical ballerina and fueled my efforts to sing in choir and play violin. The music transported me to other places and the act of sitting and listening stimulated my creative brain to kick in and see the music as colors, images, light and more.

When we had children, they too were surrounded by music. In car drives or at play, and again the creative brain kicked in to produce string players, band musicians, dancers, artists and very articulate writers and speakers. Now, the youngest is attending Boston Conservatory for flute performance but plays innumerable instruments and enthusiastically embraces learning others.

The effects of music have long been lauded as a tool for emotional healing, energetic stimulation and just pure inspiration. All directed towards the feeding of the Soul and spirit of any who take the time to connect. We are surrounded by vibration, but the structure and organization of well-defined music can be stuff that lifts the ordinary into the imaginary and the creative imaginary into invention and innovation.

Spend some time this week engaged in active listening to a piece of music that just might inspire you.

Notes From the Week:

WEEK 27: Keeping It Spiritually Simple

In our attempts to connect with Spirit and the Divine, we often get bogged down with spending more time on the trappings of spiritual practice, leaving less time for the actual practice itself. There is the need for just the right cushion and mat for meditation. The appropriate incense and invocations for ritual and a litany of prayers, mantras and affirmations, all designed to make Deity take notice. In reality, all of these things, the "smells and bells" so to speak are to allow us to set off that trigger in mind and spirit that something that is not of the mundane world is about to happen.

Although there are times when all of the visuals are necessary, particularly when the sacred event involves more than your own private devotional; for the most part, in your personal sacred space, all that is needed to get the attention and connect with the Divine is **You**. **You** being fully engaged in oepning to the Divine. **You** quieting and simplifying the inner scenery so that the space of silence may be filled by the profound nature of Deity.

The road to the most complex and refined Truths is trod by the seeker who is garbed only in the vestments of his/her devotion; simple and pure faith and reverence for his/her own Higher nature.

Open this week to the simplicity of being fully engaged in your place of Spirit.

Notes From the Week:

WEEK 28: The Solar Connection

We feel the power of the sun's energy upon us daily and throughout the year. If we consider not only the physical properties of the Sun as the central planet of our solar system, but also look from a magickal and metaphysical perspective the attributes that we associate with solar energy are all pervasive in our daily experience.

The Sun is connected to the chakra (energetic center) which is located centrally within our body, the solar plexus. It is from this point that we generate and release energy. It is from this central location that we feel the beginning stirrings of the rise of that energy when we are engaged in spiritual practice. This is the place of energetic awakening and energetic return.

You could think of the solar plexus as being the sustainer (of aroused energy), the life and light bearer (energy produces light and a new state of being) and that which warms (energy produces heat) and promotes growth (energy moves us from one state of being to an expanded and enhanced state of awareness). All of these qualities being those of the work and impact of our physical Sun offering its strength from above.

Spend some time this week out in the sunlight. Visualize the sun enlivening the spark of the Divine Sun within you.

Notes From the Week:

WEEK 29: Finding the Still Point

There is a space within you that stands as the constant stabilizer, anchored both from the heavens and from the earth itself. There is a point within you from which all source of power and strength radiates outward. There is a point of stillness within you from whose birthing waters emotions are catalyzed by will and ripples excite the nerve endings in anticipation of something unknown.

This place of stillness will not be found in any anatomy book and cannot be removed by any ill-placed action or negative thought. It remains steady, strong and sure, connecting you to the webbing of all life. There are times when this stillness is tested and shaken, but it will not falter, even when you will it into the frenetic dance of disequilibrium.

And, it is in these chaotic times that the stillness becomes all pervasive, which gives the illusion of it having abandoned you at the time of greatest need. It is this stillness that moves you to learning the necessary lessons of anchoring and rooting yourself more firmly so that the storm may blow as it will as you remain like the supple willow that bends in surrender.

As you move through your week, try to give awareness to those opportunities for you to remain anchored and still. Search out the point of stillness within you. Feed it the intent of strength and fill it with the light of balance.

Notes From the Week:

WEEK 30: Bridging Beliefs

There is a saying I firmly believe that declares that all (positive) spiritual paths ultimately lead to the One (source of all)synthesized Path. My belief in this has come as the conclusion of countless numbers of years exploring many different belief systems. From these explorations the threads of commonality, albeit different semantics, wove a tapestry that is rich and diverse in the many roads taken.

I also firmly believe that choosing a specific spiritual path is a very personal choice and as such should be made by every individual of their own accord and in their own time. When we reach out to obtain more information about the varied beliefs, we are better informed about what our own belief system looks like. When we take the time to participate in some of these rites and ceremonies of worship, we can feel at a deeper level what resonates for our own practice.

And, if after having decided on our own course we maintain the effort at bridging the divide that often occurs when we only see from the narrow lens of our own perspective, and remain open to what each spiritual path has to offer the other, we become the bridge under whose strength the many streams to the One may flow.

This week do a little research into a spiritual path other than your own. What are the commonalities and what are the differences?

Notes From the Week:

WEEK 31: What Moves You?

What gets you fired up and ready to go? What motivates your desires and fuels your needs? What propels you to a place of greatness and appreciation of your self-worth? What are the things that excite you and make you want to give your best? What picks you up and lifts your spirits when you are feeling less than your best?

What moves you to the point of tears because of the sheer beauty of that place, person or object? What makes you want to reach out and draw someone closer to you? What inspires you to produce something that is creative and useful? What angers you and brings you to the point of being less than kind and at times downright cruel?

What makes you continue to want to thrive and live a life filled with love and abundance? What do you see reflected back at you in the eyes of a loved one? What do you see of yourself, in someone you despise? What sets your mind on fire with invention and bright idea?

And, as you sit communing with your Higher Self in the quiet space of the Divine, think back to the question of what moved you to this profound moment.

Notes From the Week:

WEEK 32: In Gratitude

If you were raised as I was, you were taught to say "thank you' when receiving something, to be grateful when someone does you a favor, and especially at Thanksgiving to offer up with great verbosity the laundry list of gratitude to family and friends.

Now, I am not saying that these things are not good models of polite behavior, but as with many things to which we are conditioned, we act and react on auto-pilot without giving much thought to what the words really mean. With that being said, the challenge then becomes to bolster each word, action and offering of gratitude with the full understanding and intent that it rightfully deserves.

Now, you would think that holding these standards would lessen those grateful moments, but the surprising thing is that when we truly are grateful for what has been given us, we see more clearly the abundance of things we can offer up gratitude to. A good beginning to this is to start a gratitude journal.

Each night before going to bed, list the things for which you have given deep thought and are truly grateful for their presence. It does not matter how small or short-lived that thing was, just write it down. As you continue this process, you will become more selective in what is deserving of thanks and also see areas of your life that would have gone unnoticed and remained lacking a state of gratitude.

Notes From the Week:

WEEK 33: The Work of Community

We dance the circle
And move to
Rhythmic drum
Each connected to the other
A tribe, a gathering
A weaving into one.

Time moves the Great Wheel
We lift our spirits high
And in celebration we declare
We are the community.

We are those who serve and
It is our Great Mother
Upon which
In unity we stand.

Strong in our connections
Mind, body and hearts in sync
Father Sun's passion
Flames at our central core.

Voices raised in joy
And love as
Hands create and heal
Our magickal work never done.

And so in perfect love and trust
We embrace the Path ahead
The Greater work of our community
First steps, first paths now blaze strong
Enlivened by more than one.

What is your work within your spiritual community?
What is your work in the tribe of your making?

Notes From the Week:

WEEK 34: The "Anytime" New Year

December 31st marks the last day of the calendar year and we bring all the accumulated lessons, joys and sorrows of that year with us as we cross the threshold into a new beginning- the first day of a new year. For many, this self-initiated new start is welcomed by the making of carefully and thoughtfully chosen "resolutions". And, just as many, often find that by the end of that cyclic year, those resolutions have fallen by the wayside, replaced by regrets or excuses for not having accomplished what we had set out to. What I would like to offer is a new way of looking at this yearly ritual.

In fact, we can get the process off to a good start by thinking and approaching it as a sacred act, complete with inspired intent and focused will that may serve to enhance the determination needed to sustain you throughout the entire year. Additionally, we can take this approach and make any day the start of our own personal "new year".

Select your special day and as you sit and pen your "resolutions", take a moment to pause and breathe with intent into those things you wish to release and to bring into your life. Take some time to open to all the possibilities that these new intentions offer up.

What do you resolve to transform? And, what strength of resolve will you bring to creating your own "New Year"?

Notes From the Week:

WEEK 35: The Hunger

What aches within you to know the Divine.
What fills your table of spiritual sustenance.
To what ends will you go to sit at the table
Of your Divine Nature.

Does this hunger awaken you at night, calling you to sit
In sacred space and open to the silence of Spirit.
Do you feel sorrow at grains of wisdom spilled out
From bowls upturned in frantic search.
Do the rumblings of your belly and physical need
Distract you from the call to dine at the table of the
Most Divine.

I will feed this hunger with words of inspiration.
I will sit with others in wait and accept what
offerings Are given, in gratitude and love.
I will take from my plate and feed those who have not
The will, that they may know the bounty that is theirs.

I will quiet this hunger, but not completely.
For it is within that empty space that I will grow my
Devotion and gather strength to nourish me on this
Path of service.

I will feed this hunger so that it may grow, and be sated
By the gnosis of my own table of Divine offerings.

How will you feed your spiritual nature this week?

Notes From the Week:

WEEK 36: In A Perfect World

The quest for perfection pervades our society. The perfect job, home, body, relationship, children, etc. This is not limited to our mundane pursuits. It spills over into our spiritual life. The perfect spell, mantra, prayer, energetic protocol, meditative technique- all in the hopes of propelling us towards enlightenment and ascension.

Perfection is a state of mind. It is what fuels us to better our game and reach a little higher with each effort made. And, the greater truth is that no matter how hard we try, perfection is elusive at best and a brutal taskmaster at worst. As I have matured and thought more deeply about the striving for perfection (I was a ballet dancer after all, so nothing was ever good enough), I have come to realize that the existence of a perfected world and perfected state would be very inert. The goal having been achieved and not anything higher to aspire towards; apathy and stagnation are the norm. And, what was deemed as perfect, would very quickly succumb to mediocrity and decline.

So, I will embrace my less than perfect state and allow the fires of aspiration to move me on towards a loftier goal of change and chalk up those less than perfect efforts as the lessons that transformed me the most.

What endeavors will you willingly allow to fall just short of perfect?

Notes From the Week:

WEEK 37: The Eye of the Needle

It takes a certain amount of skill, keen eyesight and a steady hand to thread a sewing needle. The eye is usually too small and without adequate lighting it is like searching in the dark for the light switch; knowing exactly where it is, but missing the mark every time. But, without this precious thread, the work of sewing and creating cannot be accomplished.

Maintaining a spiritual practice can at times replicate the scenario above. The thread is your accumulated efforts that are trying to be guided through the narrow gateway of actual progress so you may do the work of your path. The steady hand that is needed requires commitment to a routine that then becomes a habit, and ultimately blends seamlessly into the fabric of your life, both mundane and spiritual. The keen eyesight required is seeing with selective intent in choosing those practices that will enhance and support your spiritual life and being ruthless about trimming away those that are not.

The test of skill is how effectively you balance both your mundane and spiritual pursuits, aiming ever for the goal of them becoming interactive and interwoven one into the other. And, when all has been readied and aligned with the eye of the Gateway, these golden threads that have been carefully spun will glide smoothly through the stillness of the center point emerging on the other side, ready to do the work at hand.

Notes From the Week:

WEEK 38: The Law of Silence

I often speak in my teachings about the power of the Silence. The energy of that pause between what is exhalation of word and inhalation to gather together the next verbose outpour. It is within that sacred space of pure absence of sound (vibration) that the quickening begins.

Think of a gate. Each side of the central opening must be solid and supportive in nature to receive the outward push that is exerted by what lay in the mid-space. It also serves as an interface on either outer edge; remaining strong and supportive of what is pushing in on it. The tension that is needed for the supports to remain supportive comes from that open space that is the gateway between. It has the vantage point of being both a receiver and a distributor. Within its space of structure the energies may gather together from either edge of support and intermix in a way that creates entryway into another space.

In the reading of certain spiritual works, the import lies in what is said between the lines of the writing. It is that open space between the lines of sentence where the keys of mystery are held and can be revealed only when you linger long enough for them to be revealed.

Carve out your own space of silence this week. Listen to what is being said in the pause between the words. Take note of the space of silence, and listen intently.

Notes From the Week:

WEEK 39: Honoring the Ancestors

The Honoring of the ancestors is a theme that has long held sway in the months of October's end and November's beginnings. Even if you are not overtly looking for that connection, the air at that time of the year feels somehow denser; more crowded and alive with an undercurrent of energy that is quite different from that of the summer or winter months.

In most of the cultures throughout the world, there is a time, space and ritual associated with paying respect to the ancestors.

Setting aside a special date and starting a tradition of remembering our loved ones who have passed can create a deeper connection to our heritage and the energies and lives that went into the creation of who we are today. Whether our family life was idyllic, dysfunctional or somewhere in between, the interactions we had with the people in our lives has formed and shaped us. If we take it back further and do some research into our grandparents, more of our own nature is revealed. We also see more clearly what effects this past had on those who nurtured us. This lineage is our gift and taking time to honor those who shared that gift is a beautiful form of keeping alive their memory.

Plan a specific date to hold the memories of your past loved ones in a place of honor and gratitude.

Notes From the Week:

WEEK 40: A Beautiful Garden

What seeds have you planted lately? It may be the middle of the coldest winter, but we can still have a beautiful garden. This is the garden that lies within and needs weeding, tending and harvesting just as the outer garden requires these same things.

Each thought or inspiration we have is a seed of idea that can be brought to fruition or remain the stuff of daydreams. Every emotion we have warms or deadens what our responses or reactions will be in any given interaction. Every action we take is in the form of either weeding and refining or destroying and laying waste to what was germinated.

When we align our mind with right action and feed it with emotion and intent that is guided by our higher self, our garden will thrive and grow. Each seed that is planted will be done so with care and nurtured so that it may reach the ripeness of its full potential. The necessary release will come in the form of the harvesting of those rare fruits of spiritually empowered effort and action. And, all with whom you interact will reap the benefits of your bountiful nature.

As you go about your business of daily activity give some time and planning towards the creation of an inner garden. Select its seeds as carefully as you would from a catalogue for a Spring outdoor planting. And, then begin the sowing of what will be your beautiful garden.

Notes From the Week:

WEEK 41: A Stellar Find

One of the greatest keys to our spiritual development lay in the blueprint of our natal chart. The planets, signs and houses all have their own stories and mysteries of potential to be revealed. I began my study of astrology by analyzing and looking at my own chart, piece by piece. Although there is much to be learned if you want to become proficient at understanding astrology the journey can be fascinating and enlightening.

Begin by obtaining a copy of your natal chart. Take a look at your Sun, Moon and Ascendant (Rising) signs. Then dig in and do some reading about each of the astrological signs of those three components above. When you have adequate information move on to looking at the other planets and their signs in your chart. Read about each planet's core energy and what that means in your particular blueprint. As you begin to learn more about yourself and the places where you hold the most potential, you can begin to formulate ways to enhance those strengths and minimize the weaknesses.

There are several sites on line that allow you to generate your own birth chart with some basic information. This week, check out your own stellar blueprint and then explore the workings of the cosmos within you. Bring the Astrological Wheel to life as you stand as the solar center.

Notes From the Week:

WEEK 42: Time Matters

As members of a modern society, we are driven by time. Just about everything in our lives is scheduled and bound by the constraints of linear time. And, the most common complaint is that of not having enough time. The quick fix is to restructure our daily schedule to be inclusive of all the things that need to be accomplished. This often makes for feelings of being more bound by time, with even less wiggle room. As a busy mother of five when my children were little the very thought of scheduling time for myself, set me into panic. How would I ever have time to schedule time to make time?

I have come to the realization that time marches forward in its own pace regardless of what tricks we try to apply to deceive it. And, that the best approach is one of being self-centered. Not in the sense of disregarding everyone else's needs, but in the action of being fully present in what I am currently doing. Allowing time to move around **me** as the pivotal center point that is held in the moment and not carried in the timely undertow.

Surprisingly, as soon as I changed my way of thinking about time, there seemed to be a bit more of it. And, yes there are some time issues that you have no control over, but generally I seemed to finally have enough time to accomplish what I wanted with time to spare to be spontaneous in how I used it.

So, how will you mange your time more effectively and remain self-centered this week?

Notes From the Week:

WEEK 43: Polishing the Stones

Have you ever noted at the marvel of how stones and rocks in a stream have been smoothed by the continual flow of water over their surface. At times, this water is gentle in current and at others flowing full force and transforming what was jagged and rough edges to those that are smooth and easier to move through.

Our emotions can serve the same purpose if we allow the flow to be purposeful and directed in its course. The stones of jagged edges that we hold within where forgiveness can not pass easily or anger rips to shreds any gentle thought can all be smoothed so that the current may continue on its course.

Imagine within yourself a river of healing waters flowing through every part of your body. Pick a point of focus and in your mind's eye travel along the flow of this river as it meanders through you. Pause at each blockage or jagged stone that tries to impede this flow of healing. Take a closer look at what energy it holds and what detail has been carved into is surface. Breathe into the waters that surround it and see them rise and move with force and intent over the edges and surface of this stone. Feel the soothing and smoothing action of this force and flow. Now, see behind you this same stone, no longer with jagged edges protruding. See the waters flowing gently and unimpeded over its surface. See it smooth and polished gleaming with the luminosity and power of the healing waters. Which of your stones are in need of polishing?

Notes From the Week:

WEEK 44: Release Me

I step cautiously into the current of waters
That would carry me forward.

Fear of losing ground and being pulled
Beneath water's surface holds me on the
Banks of perceived safe ground.

So, I stand, ever the observer looking
Out onto a horizon that can only
Be revealed in its beauty
To those who simply let go.

I step into my skin and look down
At water's mirrored surface.
I will not turn away from reflection
Cast of face and rippling form.

I will not look beyond the surface
Of that physical form
And vow to open a compassionate
Heart to myself staring back.

I strain and push against a container
Never fitting quite right.
I hover just above, never settling in
Poised, as always in control.

For now, this will prove enough.
I am not ready to face the icy waters of reality.
I am not ready to be released.

What holds you captive and what will you choose to release so that you may flow with the current of life?

Notes From the Week:

WEEK 45: Shower of Light

Use your morning shower to illuminate and energize your day. Visualize the droplets of water as luminescent beads of pure light. As they move over your body, feel the core of their essence as being filled with healing, active and productive energy. See yourself flowing through your day with grace and as easily as the water flows over your body. No resistance or impediment, simply gentle, moving flow descending from above and grounded in the foundation of earth. Breathe into this light and allow it to envelope you covering you head to toe in protection, appropriate energy and strength.

If you shower in the evening before bed, visualize these beads of light as gently soothing and calming anything that was disruptive and unproductive in your day. As they move over your body, visualize any stresses, concerns or worries falling away from you, purified and transformed into positive and productive essence for a good night's rest. Feel the warmth and healing properties of the water connecting with you at your emotional level, allaying any fears you may have. Breathe into this light and allow it to envelope you covering you head to toe in protection, healing and serenity.

Try this visualization for the week as you shower each day. Make note of any greater ease in navigating your day and/or improved sleep.

Notes From the Week:

WEEK 46: Devoted to Your Practice

There are many ways to express devotion within your spiritual practice. Setting up an Altar dedicated to whatever vision you have of the Divine is a beautiful way to display your dedication and devotion. Acknowledging your Spiritual Path and the work you have achieved on that Path as you sit in contemplative medication is an affirmation of your Devotion.

Each time you spend a moment in thought about the magick that surrounds you, the marvel of your physical body and give thanks for those others who share your life generates the energetic pattern of Devotion. An act of kindness or gentle word offered up at just the appropriate time is devotional in its nature of recognizing the need in another. Seeing reflected in yourself the potential to affect all that surrounds you in a positive and constructive way is offering up devotion to Divinity and acknowledging the Divine within you.

Just as a perfectly formed rose has many petals, each wrapped and integrated within the space of the other, there are many devotional paths of your creation that are unfolding at any given moment. Some are hidden and others are there for all to see. But, all lead to the very center and heart of the flower. And it is by ever striving towards that center that we find the many ways that devotion forms and shapes our lives.

What form does Devotion take within your spiritual path?

Notes From the Week:

WEEK 47: The Fear of Success

For many people their greatest fear is that of failure. We strive to do our best and hope that our efforts will be declared a great success. And, when we fall short of that mark, we often spiral into self-blame, humiliation, excuse giving and frustration that our best wasn't good enough.

I would propose that there is more to lose when we actually succeed at something. When you are declared competent and successful in an endeavor, there is now the pressure to maintain that success and competency. There are no adequate excuses that can be given as to why success has not remained an ally. When we fail at something, there is always the greater lesson to be had in that process, even if it is not apparent at the time. When we succeed, we look at it as the final achievement and don't always push ourselves beyond that success because we feel there is no need to.

My proposal is that there should be no fear, nor hesitancy in achieving either status. The degrees to which one fails or succeeds are floating targets at best. And, neither should be the final determiner of whether we move forward or remain complacent with the results. I would strive to turn the perspective around and see both states as learning opportunities from which we continue to move, change direction and grow. What success do you fear, and what is the lesson to be learned by their failure?

Notes From the Week:

A 5-minute Meditation to Renew and Restore

Find a space where you will not be disturbed for approximately 5 minutes Take a few deep breaths *(pg. 55/Wk.24)* using the Four fold breath technique. Sink deeper into your space of physicality. Allow each breath to draw you inward. Turn your attention to the point within where you feel most centered. It may be at the place of your solar plexus, your sacral area of your mid chest. Breathe into this space with fully present awareness. Imagine a small golden pearl of light glowing centrally within the space of your centered awareness. Allow this pearl to expand with each exhalation. The golden glow growing and now warming this central space. Continue with this gentle pace of breath and the expansion of the golden glow of light until it fills the entirety of your central space of awareness. Feel its energy radiating out and into your extremities, torso and trunk. Feel the heat and strength that it emanates outward, filling your being with enlivened and renewed energy. Simply breathe into this feeling for a few minutes. Each breath strengthening the dynamics of its energy and brightening its light. Take one large breath in and visualize this expanse folding into itself and shrinking back to a small pearl like dot. Take another deep breath in drawing the entirety of it back into your center point. Gently flutter your eyes open and resume your activities for the day. Do this daily for the week.

Notes From the Week:

WEEK 49: The Heart of the Matter

May I be a vessel of Light as we slowly transform.

May I be a vessel of Love as time moves swiftly ahead.

May I be a vessel of strength and offer refuge to anchor and ground.

And, may each step I take be in service to the Divine Will of Spirit.

These words were gifted to me during a meditation to open myself to compassion. I am an Aquarian who is very logical and very much in my head. Part of my spiritual work has been to connect more fully with heart-centered action, and put mental processes in the background. I am continually working on this. Working to breathe into the heart center and moving more naturally and in rhythm with the emotional flow.

In order to be more fully open to the heart I must first acknowledge the physical being in which this spiritual love resides. This is the space of matter that contains both the physical and spiritual heart. Using the interface of mind has brought deeper understanding of the intricacies of a mind-heart dialogue.

In claiming my physical self, I can more fully engage the spiritual; all parts of it and most especially the heart center of compassionate Love.

Make effort this week to act from heart-centered motivation.

Notes From the Week:

WEEK 50: Standing Your Ground

Holding a grounded attitude throughout your day allows you to remain flexible and centered regardless of the discordant energies around you. Below is a simple grounding technique that can be used anywhere at any time of the day.

Stand with your feet placed firmly and directly underneath your hip-bones with knees slightly bent and relaxed. Your spine is elongated and your shoulders are relaxed with your head resting gently on top. Bring your awareness to the rhythm of your breath; the filling of your lungs and the gentle exhale. Each exhalation releases another bit of tension from the day's activities. As you continue to breathe, imagine a line of energy connecting you to the ground beneath the floor on which you are standing. Each breath in draws the grounding energy from the Great Mother up into your being. This energy of life moves progressively upwards, moving through your feet into the lower legs, up into the pelvic region, up into the belly, up into the heart center, the throat and finally passing up and through the crown chakra. As you continue to draw this energy upwards, it extends towards the sky above. Imagine that you are like the branches of a tree.

You feel wholly and completely connected to the grounding of the earth and the limitless expanse of sky above. Breathe in this energy and breathe out a cascading flow of energy that anchors you as you move through your day.

Notes From the Week:

WEEK 51: Finding Your Place of Creation

As humans we are filled with creative energy. We don't always recognize it as such, but without exception every thought, action and feeling you have has been crafted and created from that pool of energy. Recognizing the origins of this source and formulating a plan for execution that is defined, directed and intentional are the keys to being an active and engaged participant in the creative process. What comes to actual manifestation and what remains creative wish are a combination of Mind, Will, Heart and Concrete Action.

Mind: Begin by giving some thought to something that you want to manifest in your life. Think on how you will go about this process. Be very specific and detailed about what that thing will be in its finished stage. If it is a goal in the future, think about what the time line would be leading up to completion.

Will: Write in your journal each step you will take towards that goal. Plan it out in as much detail as possible. Infuse the words with your passion and desire to create. Feel the energy pour forth from your will to enliven and ignite what as been written into action.

Heart: Read through what you have written and think on how you have taken a formless idea and put it into a concrete, written form. Imbue it with gratitude and emotional strength. Imagine how completion will feel.

Now, begin the creative process and take the **physical Action** necessary to bring it into manifestation.

Notes From the Week:

WEEK 52: Coming Full Cycle

The natural order of all things works in accord with the cyclical nature of beginnings and endings. This week marks the completion of a full year's experience of looking at life from a different and varied perspective. As we celebrate the conclusion of efforts well done, we also prepare for the next cycle of beginning a new course of focus, activity and spiritual endeavor.

Go back and look through the note pages following each week. Note the highlights and which activities spurred you on towards something new. Be sure to also acknowledge those efforts given that may not have been as productive as you may have wished, and reflect on what could have been done differently. Give validation to the fact that you simply may not have resonated with some of the musings.

Going through these steps is an important part of this cycle and is the bridge of transition that occurs at every ending; just prior to a new beginning. It is the space of analysis, and being fully present in experiencing what has been left behind through achievement.

As you move the cycle of a new year, create your own habit of weekly reflection. Be open and alert to everything around you. Look for opportunities to be fully present in your actions, thoughts and emotions. Acknowledge your successes and failures; offering up the space of gratitude to the Divine for the many blessings and gifts that are inherent in every cycle.

Notes From My Year:

Notes From My Year: *(contd.)*

About the Author

Robin Fennelly is a third degree initiate within The Assembly of the Sacred Wheel Tradition and is High Priestess of Oak and Willow Coven within the ASW. Her spiritual journey is strongly rooted in both Eastern philosophy and the Western Magickal systems from which she has formed a core foundation that is diverse in knowledge and rich in spiritual practice.

As a teacher of esoteric studies, she has used Astrology, Hermetic Qabala, Numerology, and Tarot as the foundation of her diverse selection of workshops and writings for more than 20 years. Robin has written articles for The Witches' Voice online community, The Esoteric Tymes e-newslettter and her blog, The Magickal Pen. She recently completed the first two volumes of The Inner Chamber Series; *It's Written in the Stars (Astrology)* and *Poetry of the Spheres (Qabalah).*

Robin is the owner of Holistic Embrace services for mind, body and spirit and provides services such as Tarot readings, Astrology reports, Serenity Nights and other related offerings. She lives in Eastern Pennsylvania and her life is blessed by a 35-year marriage, five children, 2 pets and the opportunity to work in the field of public education.

Contact Information

Website: robinfennelly.com
Email: oawhighpriestess@yahoo.com

Books by Robin Fennelly

The Inner Chamber: Volume One
It's Written in the Stars
A Study of Astrology
First Edition: November 2012

The Inner Chamber: Volume Two
Poetry of the Spheres
Qabalah
First Edition: November 2012

A Weekly Reflection
Musings for the Year
First Edition: December 2012

Coming in 2013:

A Weekly Reflection
Musings for Another Year